First Edition

Written by Jeff Lower, Copyright 2007
Illustrations, Copyright 2007, Pegi Ballenger

First Printing
07 08 09 10 9 8 7 6 5 4 3 2 1

ISBN 10: 1-886028-87-7
ISBN 13: 978-1-886028-87-6

Library of Congress Catalog Card Number: 2007926310

Published by:

Savage Press
P.O. Box 115
Superior, WI 54880

Phone: 715-394-9513
E-mail: mail@savpress.com
Web Site: www.savpress.com

Printed in Canada

Kat's Magic Bubble

Jeff Lower

Illustrated by Pegi Ballenger

DEDICATION

This book is dedicated to Kat's little brother, Willie.

— With love, from Dad

ACKNOWLEDGMENTS

I would like to thank all of the hospital staff at the Minneapolis Children's Hospital and the University of Minnesota Hospital, especially the nurses who care for chronically ill kids as their own. Some of them will never have children of their own after all of the sorrow they have seen.

I also want to thank the people at Savage Press who saw the beauty in a tragic story.

And to Pegi, who brought that beauty out in her illustrations.

CONTENTS

INTRODUCTION

My daughter, Katherine Lacy—we called her Kat—was born with a deformed heart. She was baptized in the hall of a hospital on the way to Life Flight on the third day of her life. She was airlifted to Children's Hospital in Minneapolis, Minnesota. Kat's mom, Mary, and I raced to the Children's Hospital as quickly we dared. There, we were told of the seriousness of Kat's condition and the need for immediate surgery.

Kat was a fighter from the beginning, and after ten long days, we left the hospital with our precious little girl.

Periodic checkups were the norm. Kat did better than anyone had hoped. The doctors told us that she would always be slow and behind the other kids, but she was so far ahead in many other ways.

Then came the second operation. It was a nightmare, but Kat pulled through again. For three months, we arrived at the waiting room early each morning on her surgery days before everybody else; watched the room fill up, watched everybody leave with their kids, watched the second shift come, and watched them go. The hospital staff would tell us to shut the lights off when we left; the janitor would come and clean the room. Then the first worn-out surgeon would come in and tell us Kat was still in surgery. At the end of the fourth month, we set all of her hospital balloons free and joyously brought her home.

For a while our family enjoyed a beautiful time together. Walking down the sidewalk, enjoying the changing seasons... A little brother to share everything with arrived in the spring. Swimming, fall, Halloween, Christmas, winter...Kat loved it all!

Then came the third operation. It was to take ten days if all went well. It didn't. Seven months and countless surgeries later, we were still at the hospital. And Kat was still with us.

The doctors told us she needed a heart transplant, and we were sent to a different hospital where we waited for seven more long months.

I wrote the following stories for Kat while we were in the hospital for a period of one year. Most of it was written in her hospital room during the time before the sun rose and the hospital woke up. The stories are meant to give any child an adventure of the mind and hope in their heart while coping in an environment of doubt.

It's written to be seen through the eyes of a child, so let your imagination take you out of the hospital and into *Kat's Magic Bubble.*

— Jeff Lower

The Awakening

There was a little girl in the hospital. She had been there such a very long time and was often quite bored with doing the same things all the time. Sometimes at night she would pretend to sleep so nobody would bother her. When awake, she was very seldom left alone because of all the people trying to take good care of her.

This new night seemed the same as all the rest. But after her mommy kissed her goodnight and she rolled over to go to sleep, things were not the same. There was a faint golden light under the covers with her! At first she thought there must be a flashlight on in her bed. After going farther under the covers, she came upon the most remarkable sight. There before her was a young girl no bigger than Kat's hand. This girl glowed with a golden light and it

looked like it was snowing glitter around her. One other amazing thing was that she flew out from under the covers and hovered above the bed with a pair of very pretty wings that were attached to her back and were almost as tall as she was. The tiny girl's wings beat very fast and made a humming sound as she bobbed up and down and to and fro.

Kat at first was quite startled and didn't know whether she

should try to run or call for a nurse. She decided to grab the light; maybe it was a flashlight of some kind. When she reached for it, however, the little creature was so fast, Kat missed! Then Kat heard a little voice that said, "Don't try to catch me or I will fly away. I'm a fairy. My name is Tabby."

Now, Kat had heard of fairies and other magical creatures; however, up until now, she thought they were just pretend. "Are you a real fairy?" she asked.

"I'm a fairy princess of the northern fairies," replied the little ball of sparkling light.

"Do you live by my house?" Kat asked, hoping for a connection to her home, because she missed her home and the comfort she once had while there.

"No, I come from much farther away. We live up in the land of little trees where no people live."

The girl, enchanted with her new friend, beamed with excitement while watching the princess floating in front of her. "Can you play with me?" she asked.

"I would like that," the princess said, "but I've been here all day. Now I have to leave."

"How come nobody saw you if you were here all day?" Kat asked, a little suspiciously.

"I'm a fairy princess," Tabby exclaimed proudly, as if that were enough explanation, "and there's a lot of magic in me. Long ago when God gave humans their power over animals, their ability to see most magic was taken away. God knew that to have power over animals and see the magic in the world as well would be very dangerous for humans. I'm very hard to see in the light, and I am invisible at night if I don't move."

"I will miss you when you are gone," Kat said, her broad smile fading a little for the first time.

The fairy princess hovered for a second, then slowly said, as if thinking aloud, "I've been watching you for some time. I know you are gifted with loving kindness and see the magic in the world better than most. I will let you come with me if you want to."

"Oh, I would like that very much," said Kat in a little-girl whisper, trying to imitate the fairy princess' little voice. But a doubtful expression soon replaced the one of wonder and excitement as she realized she could not leave her room. "I can't go with you," she said, in a much sadder little whisper. She pointed to the tube in her throat, called a trach tube, and the other tubes surrounding her small body. "I'm not like other little girls. I have a breathing machine, and my legs are still too weak to let me stand by myself." Then in an even sadder voice, but a little louder, like she had just made up her mind, she said, "No, I'll just stay here and go to sleep."

"No need to worry, special one, for there's magic to spare tonight," exclaimed Tabby, shooting up a little bit and standing on her tiptoes while she glowed a little brighter and sparkled a little more, for she was very proud to be a magic fairy princess.

Then Kat felt herself rising up and the covers falling away. She was floating above her bed inside a clear bubble. This bubble was just like the bubbles she loved to blow in her bathtub, only much, much bigger. Moving and shimmering this way and that, the bubble slowly moved toward the window. Then, magically, Kat and the bubble floated through the window and they were outside and free!

The bubble began to drift with the wind away from the hospital, and soon they were up higher than the tallest trees around.

Kat squealed with delight, feeling like she was in one of the beautiful soap bubbles she loved to blow. She was lighter than air! Then Kat remembered something else about soap bubbles: They pop! "I'm up too high," she cried. "Please take me back."

Fluttering over to the front of the bubble, Tabby tried to calm her. "You are safe. I will protect you."

"But my bubble might pop."

"You have never seen a magic bubble," said the winged girl, glowing a little brighter. "Besides, it's fun to float high in the air like a bird." Then she did a quick little loop, leaving a circle of sparkling fairy dust behind and coming to a stop exactly where she had taken off.

Kat, being a very brave little girl, decided to trust her new friend. "Okay," she said, "but let's please go a little lower and not too fast."

"Watch closely; we may see some of my friends," said Tabby. The little fairy princess moved her wings very fast and opened and closed her mouth several times, talking silently to someone Kat could not see. Then she stopped talking and said, "Good, there is a northwoods troll and his flying deer close by. He will help us."

"How do you know that?" Kat exclaimed with some doubt. "I couldn't hear anything."

"People can't hear a lot of sounds in the world. It's because they can't see most of the magic around them. They can't see it, therefore, they don't understand the sounds that it makes, or they just don't hear it at all."

Kat and Tabby had drifted farther and farther from the hospital. The bubble went lower and lower. By now, Kat was content to sit and see what magic would happen next, so she was not scared when her bubble gently settled on a nearby river and began to float slowly downstream with the current.

The water gently swirled around her bubble. Tabby flew low over the water, zigzagging this way and that. Wherever she went a beautiful gold-silver color reflected up around her from the shimmering river. The rising sun was just starting to brighten the darkness when Tabby, in a dazzling ball of light, came to a stop in front of Kat's bubble.

"Can you hear it now?" asked Tabby hopefully before taking off to fly about.

"No," Kat answered thoughtfully, "all I hear is the water going by." Then the girl became sad because she wished she could fly like the fairy princess. As a matter of fact, she wished she could do the things other kids did. Kat was thinking about being different when she started to hear music. It was the most beautiful she had ever heard.

"Where is that music coming from?" Kat cried out as the music became louder and more enchanting all the time.

The fairy princess floating in front of the girl was beaming with joy. "Kat," she exclaimed, "you are a very special human. You can hear much of the magic in the world. Look carefully and you will see it, too."

The grayness of dawn surrounded her when Kat looked up and could hardly believe her eyes. Coming toward her was a wall of angels flying high above her bubble, almost shoulder-to-shoulder. Their beautiful wings were bringing them toward her rapidly. Most had long golden trumpets into which they blew, making a beautiful, enchanting melody.

Kat was staring at the angels in wonder when it happened. As the angels flew closer, she looked up and saw radiant sunbeams and the dimming starlight mixing together all around them. The angels began to glow in a beautiful golden-orange light. It was truly the most gorgeous sight she had ever seen! As they passed Kat's bubble, a curtain of light was pulled behind them so as to light up the world in a radiant early morning light. Kat turned around and watched them go, the music from their trumpets slowly fading in the distance.

Suddenly, Tabby bobbed in front of her. "Did you see them?" she questioned excitedly.

"Wow!" was all Kat could say. Then, "Yes, yes, I saw them."

Thinking about how much fun she was having and how wonderful her new friend was, she said, "Thank you for showing me all of this magic. It was beautiful."

"It's not my gift, Kat. You are the one that believes in what you see. Come on," Tabby said with a great deal of excitement, turning Kat's bubble back downstream.

Now Kat could see almost all the magic. "OH WOW" was all she could whisper, with her eyes wide open. Everything was sharp and clear. The first rays of the sun created a beautiful golden arch. She could see many fairies. Most of them were smaller than Tabby, but some were a little bigger. All were zipping this way and that, up and down, going in circles and skimming the surface of the water. The blowing fairy dust falling behind them left reflections of golden trails upon the water's mirror-like surface.

The bubble was floating close to shore now on its way down-stream. Kat could hear laughter up ahead, and on the riverbank appeared a mommy and a little boy. They were splashing their hands in a pail of water and grabbing for tiny fish.

"Will they see me?" Kat asked Tabby.

"Only people who see magic can see us this day," Tabby exclaimed, fluttering up a little to get a better look.

As Kat's bubble came up alongside them, she could hear the mommy say, "You got one!" All of a sudden the boy slipped and slid down to the river, laughing all the way.

"Mommy, look!" he said, pointing at Kat and Tabby.

"It's a little girl out for a ride," exclaimed the mommy.

"Hi," Kat called out. "I'm here to see the magic. Can you see it, too?"

"I see it every day. Where I grew up most of us learned to see some of the magic," the mommy said. Then she added, "Your bubble is very beautiful."

"Oh, thank you," Kat beamed proudly.

"I see you have a fairy princess with you. They usually just fly away from us."

"Yes. Her name is Tabby; she gave me this bubble. What are you doing with that pail?" Kat then asked, wondering what could be so much fun.

"We're trying to catch minnows so we can go fishing," the boy said excitedly, "but they're very fast and slippery."

"Yes," said the mommy, "sometimes it's more fun to play and act silly than it is to fish."

"Oh, I have to go now," said Kat, as her bubble began slowly drifting away.

"Good-bye," they both called. "Have fun today!" said the mommy as the little boy splashed his foot in the river and scampered back up the hill laughing.

As they went out of sight, Kat asked Tabby, "How could they see us? How could they see you?" Then suddenly wondering, Kat added, "Were they from Heaven?"

Before Tabby could answer, a small canoe about twice as long as Kat was tall appeared. In the canoe were five trolls and three rather large fish. All were singing in loud voices. That is, the trolls were singing, not the fish, which were probably meant for breakfast.

"Look, Tabby; look at that little boat. Don't let them pop my bubble," Kat said pleadingly, because the men scared her a little. They did indeed look strange. All except one had long hair and bushy beards. They were dressed in leather and fur clothing. Two even had tails sticking up behind them.

Tabby laughed gaily. "We're okay," she said. "They are my friends, the northwoods trolls."

By now, the canoe was landing on the riverbank. The little men were getting out and throwing their fish up on the shore.

Kat then looked around and could hardly believe her eyes. All around under the bushes along the riverbank were trolls, young and old. All were dancing and singing merrily. Small fires and tents were scattered around with everything imaginable hanging from clotheslines and trees here, there, and everywhere.

As Kat's bubble stopped on the riverbank in front of this merry group, one little fellow came down to the water's edge and seemed to start talking to Tabby, but Kat couldn't understand his language.

"This is Peakas; he is the one who will help us get back to the hospital, since the wind blew us here and I can't get us back there by myself," said Tabby. "He has a special deer named Oredy. Oredy has wings and can tow your bubble back."

Kat was very excited to see a deer that could fly. However, she was also entranced with the scene before her. "Can we stay a little while and watch?" she asked.

As if the trolls heard her, they began to come down to the river. Some had musical instruments she had never seen before. When they began to play them, a lively and beautiful sound filled the air. Other trolls grabbed sticks they used to tap to the rhythm against other sticks, small pots, or whatever they had. To all of this activity was added dancing by young and old alike.

Kat was laughing and beaming with delight. She began to bob up and down, dancing to the music as best she could while remaining in the magic bubble. Her bubble was making many ripple rings, echoing out into the glasslike river which was reflecting the early morning light up and under the bushes and making a happy and golden sight for all.

The music and dancing continued for some time before the trolls slowly began moving off to tend to the camp chores. Kat was still having a good time, but was starting to get a little sleepy, when she saw Peakas coming back leading three little deer, one of which had wings that were flapping slowly by her side.

"Here comes Oredy the flying deer," said Kat excitedly to Tabby, who was now sitting with Kat inside the bubble.

Suddenly, Tabby said, "We must hurry back," for she had lost track of the time.

Kat watched as Tabby sprinkled her bubble with a little magic fairy dust.

As they took off, Kat turned and called out, "Good-bye everybody and thank you!"

Everyone in the jolly little camp stopped their cooking and packing to turn and wave, then called out in return.

"What did they say?" Kat asked Tabby as they began floating up and over the river.

"They were saying good-bye and come back again."

With Oredy gently towing the bubble, Kat enjoyed the ride back to her room. She was proud of her new friend, the magic fairy princess, so she felt very sad when her exciting adventure ended and her bubble slipped back through her hospital window. Soon, she was nestled back under the covers. As she pulled her covers up, she realized the bubble had disappeared. She hadn't felt it vanish.

"Don't be sad," Tabby comforted the sleepy little girl. "We had fun today."

"Yes, we did," said Kat, yawning. "Will you come back?"

"Yes, and soon. I like you very much," answered Tabby.

Kat smiled and closed her eyes to rest. And nobody in the

hospital knew she had been away, floating inside a magic bubble with her new friend Tabby, the fairy princess.

The Gift

Spring passed and summer arrived. Kat and Tabby have had many talks and outings since their first adventure together. One day, Kat sat in her chair looking out of her fifth floor hospital window. The sky was so blue, the sun so bright, and the young green grass of early summer so inviting. Kat sadly wondered why she couldn't go home with Mommy and Daddy to the way things used to be.

While she sat there, the doctors walked into the room next to hers. Her new neighbor was there. The doctors were going to help the little girl with her exercises, or as Kat called it, P.T., physical therapy.

Kat knows the girl's name is Crystal. She was born with crooked legs and had just had another operation to help straighten them.

Sitting in her chair, Kat was able to see into the room through the big sliding glass doors. She felt bad for Crystal, because she knows how much it hurts when she worked on her own walking.

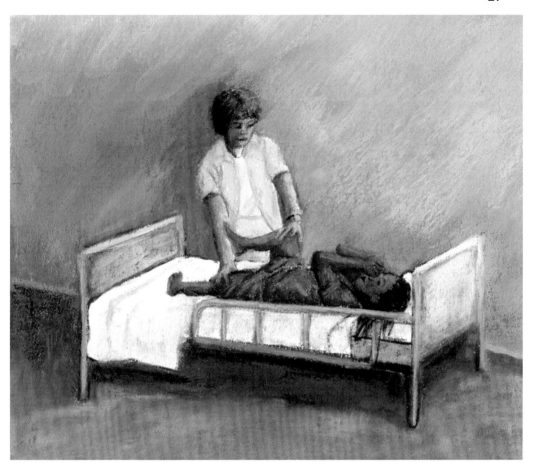

She heard the P.T. lady say gently, "Oh, Crystal. This is going to hurt a little. We have to do it though, so your legs will start to straighten out and you can walk better."

Kat watched as they slowly pushed and pulled on Crystal's legs. Crystal did not yell or scream or cry, but just said, "Owy Owy Owy," over and over the entire time.

Kat was kind of scared because she didn't know for sure what they were doing. So she was glad when she heard them say this was the last one.

"Owy Owy Owy Owy Owy," came the little voice from the other room.

Then Crystal was weeping softly, happy to have it over with for now.

"Would you like to sit by Kat for a while?" Kat heard Crystal's nurse say.

"Yes," was the weak response.

"Is it okay with you, Kat? Would you like Crystal to sit with you? You could watch TV together."

"Oh, yes!" was Kat's eager response. She watched as they helped Crystal into a wheelchair they set next to her just inside Kat's room.

"Do you know each other?" asked the nurse.

"Yep. We met last night," Kat said, turning her head, which allowed her to talk over the trach tube in her throat that connected to the breathing machine.

Kat always loved visiting with the other children in the hospital. Her happiness faded, however, when Crystal's first words were, "I want to go home!"

Hoping to cheer up Crystal, Kat decided to tell her about Tabby. "I have a special friend who comes to see me. We go outside and talk and play."

After another pause, Kat whispered, "She's a fairy princess and can fly and do magic."

Crystal stopped sobbing and turned to look at Kat more closely, but with a doubtful expression on her tear-streaked face.

"I do have a magic fairy princess friend," says Kat, a little hurt. "I do, I really do. She's coming here soon. We might go outside while my Mommy is washing clothes."

"Is she here now?" Crystal asked, whispering also, her eyes getting bigger as she slowly and hesitantly smiled. Crystal decided this might be a fun game of make-believe.

"No..." said Kat, looking around the room, then beaming brightly as she spied Tabby flying in through the open window and gliding toward Kat's collection of books and toys. "Yes! Yes, there she is sitting by my toys and books on the shelf."

"Hi, Tabby," Kat whispered excitedly, eyes sparkling, trying hard to maintain the secrecy of the event.

Crystal was very confused, because Kat was really acting like she was talking to somebody. Looking at Kat, she blurted out, "I don't see anything."

"She can't see or hear me. Remember, it's hard to see what you don't believe," Tabby responded while lightly floating and bobbing just off the shelf.

"Oh, but I want Crystal to meet you," Kat murmured. "She is sad today like I am sometimes."

Tabby, seeing Kat's disappointment as well as a small glimmer of belief beginning to form within Crystal, decided on a drastic action. This action was somewhat poorly timed, however. As Tabby rapidly flew off the shelf toward the girls, their nurse looked up and took a drink of Mountain Dew. Crystal and the nurse both saw the movement. Stopping in front of the girls, Tabby realized everybody could now see her. Thinking fast, she set off a huge burst of magic that lit up the room so brightly that nobody could see anything but white for a split second.

"Tabby, Tabby are you there?" Kat cried, holding out her hands.

"Yes, right here," she said, landing lightly on Kat's out-stretched hand. "I had to do something fast. When I tried to show myself to your friend, I realized your nurse could see me, too."

"I can see her now," stated Crystal, "but she looks invisible sometimes."

"You have to believe to see me," Tabby told Crystal, turning toward the young girl.

"What! Did you say something?" Crystal asked Kat, starting to dare to believe.

"Tabby says you have to believe in her," Kat explained to Crystal.

Crystal looked a little harder now. Then, seeing Tabby perched on Kat's hand with her hands on her hips, wings jutting back, and throwing off golden sparks of fairy dust that helped to light up the three happy faces, Crystal exclaimed in amazement, "Ha! She really is a fairy!"

"Yep," said Kat, smiling happily. "A magic fairy princess."

Then, the same question occurring to them simultaneously, both Kat and Crystal turned to look and see how the nurse was reacting to the fairy princess. What they saw was a most unusual sight. The nurse was staring straight at them with huge unblinking eyes, still drinking the pop. The whole can of liquid ran out of the can and down her chin and into a big puddle on the desk. Then the pop would go up in the air and back into the can, only to run down her chin and into a big puddle again. All three watched this for a while until Crystal asked, "Is she okay?"

"Yep," answered Tabby, looking very satisfied. "That's my best trick. My grandma taught it to me when I was told about Kat. Your nurse won't be able to see us for quite some time," Tabby added, laughing a little.

Kat and Crystal began to laugh, too.

"It's really good to see you. I was a little worried

you wouldn't make it, Tabby," Kat exclaimed excitedly.

"I'm late because I couldn't find the trolls to help get us back to the hospital," Tabby explained.

"Oh no!" exclaimed Kat. "I was hoping you could take us both for a little trip in the magic bubble."

Tabby paused thoughtfully, then frowned. "I thought we could go for just a short ride. There's a special place very close, and with the wind the way it is and a little magic, we should have no trouble getting back."

Crystal was looking worried, and Kat thought she might start crying again.

"It's okay. We go all the time," Kat whispered comfortingly, forgetting that she could now talk out loud. "I have a magic bubble that will float through the window."

"Yes, but the bubble isn't big enough for both of you," Tabby murmured apologetically, regretting not having enough magic to solve the dilemma.

There was a long silence before Kat whispered, "But you could bring Crystal and not me. Right?"

After a long, loving look into Kat's eyes, Tabby slowly answered, "Yes."

Kat swallowed hard, blinking back tears, but putting on a smile. "Crystal needs to see the magic, too."

"Is that okay with you, Crystal? Do you want to go on a trip outside?" Tabby asked after seeing the sincerity in Kat's eyes.

"Oh, yes! That would be fun." With that, Crystal was lifted up inside the magic bubble, and Tabby and Crystal floated through the window, leaving Kat in her chair.

"Whee, whee," was all she heard as Tabby and Crystal floated out of sight.

Kat turned around and sat there, smiling a little, and watching the nurse drink pop over and over again. She hoped Crystal

and Tabby were having fun. She was just wondering if Tabby had forgotten about the nurse, when suddenly there was Tabby hovering in front of her.

"Kat! Good news." Tabby was talking very fast, unable to control her excitement. "When we reached the troll camp, our friend Oredy, the little flying deer, was there. She came back with us to see you."

"Where?" Kat asked, her eyes bright with joy.

"Right over there," Tabby said, pointing to a little grove of trees near the hospital.

"Can I go now, too?" Kat asked hopefully.

"Yes," Tabby exclaimed. "Let's do it!" Before she finished the phrase, Kat was back in her bubble and floating through the window, thrilled to be on another great adventure.

They started floating down as soon as they left the hospital room. It looked to Kat as if they would land among the fast-moving cars on the road, but in the nick of time, the bubble was caught in the wind. Over some trees they gently drifted, then slowly descended below the lush green branches.

Kat felt very important sitting in her bubble with Tabby on her shoulder as the bubble settled on a small pond nestled among the rocks and ferns. Water ran out of the hill rising up to the road and created a little waterfall before reaching the pond. Sunlight beamed through the cascading water, making it sparkle and bubble on its way to the pond. The racing water then slowed, shimmering as it meandered amongst the shadows and pebbles.

Kat and Tabby floated to where Crystal sat on the side of the bank kicking and splashing in the water. Oredy, the little flying deer, was licking Crystal's face as she laughed and splashed. "Oh Kat, I'm so glad you let me come. It's so beautiful here."

Kat beamed happily as she saw Crystal's excitement. Just then, Kat looked into the shallow water and saw a small school of

fish. "Look!" She said with some awe, pointing. Then she looked at Tabby with some confusion.

"They're magic rainbow fish. That's why they turn colors like that. Most people don't see them," Tabby explained.

Kat understood immediately. "Crystal," she said, "you have to believe in magic to see the magic in the world."

As she said this, a beautiful rainbow fish came up and nibbled Crystal's toe, then flew up into the air in front of her, spraying her with droplets of water. The rainbow fish did not drop back into the water immediately, however, but floated in front of her flapping its flippers like wings. "I see them!" Crystal exclaimed, laughing with delight. Her face was radiant with joy as the little fish arched into a dive, leaving a small but brilliant rainbow all the way down and into the water. Two more rainbow fish leaped from the pond,

making beautiful rainbows as Crystal splashed her feet joyfully in the water.

"This is really fun," Kat told Tabby, thinking back. "I loved to go swimming when I was living at home. I wish my Mommy and Daddy could come here."

"Nobody comes here anymore," Tabby started to explain. Kat said nothing but looked up the hill to the busy road next to the hospital. "Long ago when the road was a trail, people used to stop here and rest or camp." Tabby continued as she watched Kat thinking about her words, "When it was a small road, they would stop and eat and enjoy the pond. Now nobody even slows down except to throw something out of their car windows where they think nobody will notice."

Kat wasn't listening anymore, however. She was looking at a tree covered with flower blossoms. "Why is that tree so noisy?" she asked Tabby.

Tabby looked at the tree covered with beautiful white flowers and wondered the same thing. "Let's go find out." She fluttered through Kat's bubble, pulling it with her on a golden chain of fairy magic. They floated across the water, leaving Crystal laughing and playing with the rainbow fish.

Gliding through an opening in the woods, they soon drifted under the beautiful little tree. The humming was much louder now, as they watched shadows moving quickly among the branches. Tabby dropped back into the bubble as it floated up into the flowers. Kat was a little worried as the leaves and flowers

started to penetrate inside her bubble. "Will the magic bubble burst?" One look at Tabby's excited face, however, calmed her as she remembered the wonderful things her bubble could do.

Kat blinked, then blinked again when she saw what was inside the upper branches of the flowering tree. Opening her eyes for the second time, Kat found herself surrounded by bright green leaves, sweet-smelling air, tiny white flowers, filtered sunlight, and the flitting shadows that were actually little birds busily taking sweet nectar from the flowers. The tiny birds fluttered everywhere inside and outside the bubble, their rapidly beating wings creating the now-familiar humming sound.

"They're hummingbirds," Kat burst out in an excited whisper, remembering the tiny and colorful creatures from her mommy's gardens.

"Hi Kat, hi Tabby," one little bird sang out as it hovered so close in front of them that Kat felt the little whiff of wind from its tiny wings. Tabby swooped and swirled in the bubble with their new friends.

"I didn't know you knew us!" Kat exclaimed.

"Oh yeah, you are Kat and Tabby. All of us have heard of you two. That's why we're here. All of the flowers in the area are extra sweet. They say it's because your magic together makes it this way."

"My magic?" marveled Kat. Tabby just smiled.

The little bird of many colors then darted to a flower and picked it with its long beak, bringing it back to Kat and Tabby. "Here, try some. It's the best."

Tabby took the flower in her tiny hand and sampled the nectar. "It *is* good," she said, handing it to Kat, who had a little trouble because her hand was so big compared to Tabby's.

Kat looked into the flower and saw the nectar in the bottom. She noticed the sweet smell of the flowers even more as she sipped from the tiny flower cup.

"Yum, I like it," she said, even though it was a very small taste. "Hey, let's bring some to Crystal!"

"Good idea," one little bird chirped, and flew the short distance to where Crystal had finished splashing in the water and was now watching Kat and Tabby.

"Let's go, too," Kat said to Tabby.

They reached the pond just as Crystal dropped the little flower cup into the mirror-like water, watching the beautiful petals floating above the sandy bottom.

"This is fun!" Crystal smiled and laughed. "I never knew there was so much magic so close. I can't wait to tell everybody about it when I go home tomorrow."

"Yep," agreed Kat, looking fondly at her new friend.

Tabby's tiny voice piped in a little sadly, "Yeah, but look at all those cars going by up there. We came this short distance and saw all this beauty. Everyone else went right by and didn't even see us."

****

It was dark in Kat's room. The big day was over. Kat's mommy read Kat her favorite stories and tucked her in bed. The day nurse went home, wondering why there was sticky pop all over her chin. The night nurse had arrived, listening to the steady rhythm of Kat's breathing machine. Kat lay curled up under the covers.

It was not dark everywhere, though, for in Kat's hands there was a little ball of light. It was Tabby. After they floated back through Kat's hospital window, Tabby had waited, hiding in the room. Now the hospital quieted down, and they were enjoying another nightly gab session.

"That was a wonderful gift you gave Crystal by staying here and letting her go for a ride in your bubble," said Tabby.

"It was hard, but I wanted her to see the magic, too," answered Kat.

"How did those talking hummingbirds know us?" Kat asked after a little pause

"I'm not sure," Tabby responded. Tabby was quiet for a long moment as she struggled with her long-kept secret. "I'm here for a reason. I haven't told you this before.

"After I was born, my parents began to notice that I was different. I had more magic than they did and learned very quickly. Nothing in our magic world could explain it. Then my dad looked in an old book of magic and found rare, but similar, occurrences. Mom decided I was linked with something or someone in the non-believing world, so she sent out the word to all those living in the northwoods to find out what or who I was linked with.

"We searched the whole world; even the mushroom fairies and cloud fairies helped. The trolls and the deer and the fish helped. Finally, an old, powerful gremlin wizard from the darkness was tricked into telling us what happened."

After another pause, Tabby revealed the secret to Kat. "My mom says you and I are linked. She says we were both born at the very same instant." Tabby's little voice quivered as she tried to hold back her emotions. "You see, Kat, my mom says we are sisters."

As Kat and Tabby looked at each other with love, no words were needed. They both drifted off to sleep, snuggled under the covers together, on the hot summer night.

Going Home

In Kat's hospital room, Tabby hovered at the window in the area where light mixed with shadow. Perched there next to the glass and the dark of outside, Tabby was almost invisible except to Kat, of course, who kept eyeing her with knowing glances. Kat was worried that someone might sit on her fairy princess friend, for the room was quite crowded tonight. Tabby, however, kept giving off little bursts of reassuring light and magic, which blended nicely with the thick frost of winter covering parts of the window. Strings of lights sparkled joyfully about Kat's room, adding to the concealment of Tabby's light show.

On this special night, Christmas Eve, a large gathering of people filled the room. Mommy, Daddy, and little brother Willie were there, along with all of Kat's friends from the hospital. The noise level throughout the room was an expression of the happiness and joy within. Kat sat in the middle of the room in her little kid's chair, beaming brightly and pointing to the next person whom she wanted to open a gift. Mommy and Daddy smiled, but there was sadness in their eyes as they noticed that Kat had stopped trying to talk over her breathing machine and was doing most of her communicating with body movements, smiles, eyes, and sometimes frowns.

Finally, Kat pointed to her brother, her twin in spirit and pupil in attitude. Brother Willie ripped into his gift with overdue anticipation. It was a rainbow maker like the ones she had given Mommy and Daddy on their birthdays. Willie held it up high to see the sparkles.

"You have to wait for a sunny day," Kat instructed, her voice weak but still with a big-sisterly tone.

In an unexpected move, Willie clutched the rainbow maker in his hand and ran to Kat, giving her a big hug while being extra careful not to disturb any of her medical lines. Kat beamed at Willie's happiness, and for a moment it seemed like they were back home.

So it went for the remainder of the evening, but all good things must come to an end. Everybody said goodnight, and the hospital friends left the room. Mommy and Daddy got Kat ready for bed and turned the lights down low.

"Goodnight, my treasure," Daddy murmured.

"Thank you, button nose," Mommy said as she kissed her daughter.

"I love you," Willie chimed in, adding in a whisper, "We're going to the little church for a Christmas service."

"Good-bye," Kat answered with a beautiful smile on her face.

In the nearly dark room, Kat and Tabby talked again under

the covers. Christmas music and beeping hospital monitors covered their little voices.

"I want to go, too," were the first words whispered once Kat found her little friend glowing under the covers.

After carefully considering the danger involved and with a long pause, Tabby began to speak, her wings sparkling only slightly. "I've got a present for you, too."

"Oh, can I go home like we talked about?" Kat questioned hopefully and a bit too loudly.

"Shh," Tabby hushed Kat. "Yes, but just for a little while."

Then Kat, once again inside her bubble, floated through the

window, leaving her unaware nurse behind. Once outside in the cold, crisp air, her bubble began sinking fast. Kat's fear was soon replaced with excitement, though, as both Oredy, the small flying deer, and Peakas, her troll friend, joined her. Tabby quickly connected a magic harness from Kat's bubble to Oredy, and they slowly floated upward.

"I didn't know Peakas was coming," said Kat.

"Yep," answered Tabby, sounding more than a little like Kat. "Peakas knows the way across the woods better than any other troll."

With Peakas riding on Oredy's back, they headed north toward Kat's home. Tabby fluttered all around the merry group, leaving her magic dust to fall upon the land below.

They floated silently over a little church. The glowing lights and the beautiful sounds of Christmas carols coming from below filled the night air, and Kat wondered if Tabby was teasing her and this was their real destination. Magic fairy dust began to sprinkle upon the roof of the church, allowing Kat to look inside. They watched her family hurriedly taking off their winter coats and getting seated in the back row. Kat giggled, remembering how her dad didn't like being late. Too soon, though, the magic window through the roof closed, and Oredy continued pulling them against a cold wind.

"Yes, I want to go home," Kat heard herself saying. Soon they were traveling high and fast, making good time. Flying this high was unusual for Kat and Tabby, but they were on a mission. Nobody said anything as it became colder and colder. Soon they were far past the lights and sounds of the city. Over farms and small towns they flew. Multi-colored bands of light in the sky seemed to roll and change color all around them.

"What's that?" Kat asked, pointing with a look of wonder upon her face.

"They are northern lights," Tabby explained. "I see them a lot at my home." That's all she could say without her teeth chattering from the cold.

The weather conditions were getting worse. The wind had let up, but it was bitterly cold. Kat didn't notice the worry on Peakas' face or the trouble Tabby and Oredy were having in keeping on course.

The trees were pretty close when Tabby, with tears in her eyes, exclaimed, "We can't go on." Then she paused, and everybody realized they were descending very rapidly.

Tabby's magic was gone: It was too cold for even the most powerful northwoods fairy. Without Tabby's help, Oredy couldn't hold them up, and into the trees they plummeted. As scared as she was, Kat managed to throw her weight from side to side in order to miss the tree trunks. Even so, the smaller branches breaking around them made a frightening sound. Then everything turned white as they landed in the deep, fluffy snow on the forest floor.

"Is everybody okay?" Kat heard a somewhat dazed Peakas ask as the white cloud settled back into the snowdrifts surrounding them.

Kat looked around. It was hard to see where everybody was. Eerie shadows from the northern lights shining through the branches above made monster-like hands that seemed to be grabbing this way and that.

"Where's Tabby?" she managed to ask, looking frantically around her. Finally, Oredy popped her head out of the snow.

"Where's Tabby!" Kat cried out again, louder this time. The three friends looked around, worried. Then, "Look!" Kat shouted, spying a glow coming from under the snow. "Help her out!"

Oredy nudged her nose deep into the snow, gently lifting Tabby out. She set her in Kat's hand, and Kat hugged her tightly.

"I'm sorry," Tabby managed to say. "The wind took all my magic, and I didn't know it was going to be this cold."

"It's okay," Kat murmured into the darkness, grateful that everyone was safe.

Tabby looked up at Kat, sadness on her face. "I'm sorry, " she said again. "I have to rest. Then we'll try to get back to the hospital." With that, she laid her head down, staring wearily into the woods.

Oredy struggled over to Peakas who was still trying to brush the snow out of his fur clothes. The little deer nudged Peakas, whispered in the troll's ear, then settled into the snow.

"No," Peakas answered, "you'd never make it with me on your back." Peakas' voice was shaking now with cold. "I'm not sure where the troll village is or if there are flying deer there."

"You should go by yourself," Kat said to Oredy.

Oredy slowly pushed through the snow, her wings too stiff to try to fly. Then she lay down close to Kat's bubble.

"I'll try to light a fire," Peakas whispered, pulling his dry fire makings from his pocket.

"Tabby," Kat breathed, but there was no response. "Tabby," she repeated more urgently.

A weak resply came from the half-frozen form resting in her hand. "We must wait for Peakas' fire," Tabby managed to gasp, her lips almost too cold to move.

Kat was too cold to notice that most of Tabby's delicate wings were frozen, and she was becoming invisible. Small holes in Kat's bubble were getting bigger and bigger.

They all huddled closer together as Peakas informed them the cold just wouldn't let his fire burn warmly.

Kat and Tabby looked up with fear in their eyes. The trees seemed to have faces that looked down at them. The Pop! Pop! Crack! of freezing trees was the only sound to be heard as it got even colder.

Tabby was the first to notice. "Look, everybody," she shouted, suddenly energized and bouncing up, her wings glowing fully again.

Very light flakes of snow began to drift around, weaving up and down as if they didn't know that snow must eventually hit the ground. Not one snowflake hit the forest floor, however. They were starting to swirl around Kat's bubble. Suddenly, every little puff of white started to glow with a little light from within. They started spinning around Kat as she watched in awe. In and out of her bubble they went, lifting her up off the ground. She had a strange weightless feeling. Some snowflakes brushed against her, tickling her until she did not feel cold anymore. Kat giggled and smiled, watching them weave and swirl about. Suddenly, Kat was gently set

down, and the little lights floated off in all directions and slowly faded away.

There was Tabby in front of her, standing tall and proud, her wings moving so fast as not to be seen. There was fairy dust sparkling all around them.

"That was amazing," Tabby burst out, doing a loopedy-loop in the air. "The snow fairies saved us," she said, stopping and bobbing up and down.

"Snow fairies?" Kat questioned, still feeling a little silly from all the tickling.

""Yes," said Tabby, talking fast, "snow fairies are the rarest and most powerful of all the fairies."

"Where did they go?" Kat asked, looking around.

"Snow fairies are only here for a very short time," Tabby explained.

"Will they come back?"

"No, they went back to where they came from. Sometimes the best things on earth are only here for a little while. You must be very special," Tabby stated, getting control of her excitement, "in order for the snow fairies to come and see you during their brief time here."

"You're both special," Peakas said as Kat and Tabby turned to look at him, tending his fire that had burst into flame as the snow fairies left.

The four friends sat together, feeling the warmth of the fire.

Finally, Tabby broke the companionable silence. "We have plenty of magic now, and it's not too late."

Oredy reached out and bumped Tabby with her cold wet nose, giving her a "let's go" signal. Thanks to the extra magic given to them by the snow fairies, they were soon floating high above Kat's town. Kat was thrilled to be looking down upon familiar places at last. They drifted over the frozen lake and the beach

where Kat went swimming, and the park where she had learned to swing.

Suddenly, Tabby asked, "Where would you most like to go?"

Kat looked down on the sleeping town. She remembered all the fun she had had while living at home: the birthdays, the hot summers, the cold snowy winters, the dazzling lightning storms, and all the rest of her happy memories. "I want to talk to Grandma. She lives right down there," Kat said excitedly, pointing the way.

"Okay," answered Tabby, "but you can't let her know we are

with her, and we don't have much time left to get back; it will be light soon."

Leaving Oredy and Peakas, Kat and Tabby silently drifted down through the shimmering night sky. Through a magic hole in the roof they sank. Tabby stayed in the bubble as Kat crept to the edge of her grandma's bed. Sobbing a little now, Kat wished she could cry out, "I'm here! I'm back!" But remembering not to wake her, Kat only whispered, "I'm here, Grandma. It's me, Kat." She smiled lovingly at her grandma.

Grandma stirred a little. Still mostly asleep, she whispered, "I miss you, Kat."

Kat was very happy as she softly murmured, "I will always be your little girl. Just think of me playing in your kitchen or the

backyard, and I will be here. Remember our walks and how I like rain and helping my daddy at work. Close your eyes and see me holding my smiling little brother and notice how proud I look. See, Grandma, you'll always have your little girl."

"You're so beautiful," Grandma whispered, smiling a little now.

Kat and Tabby didn't say much as they drifted high once again over forests, lakes, and small towns. They were content with the wonder of it all. It truly was a silent night.

Kat was asleep when they reached the city, her hands in her lap, gently holding the sleeping Tabby. As they passed over the little church, the bubble broke free from Oredy's magic harness and floated down. Kat and Tabby sank onto the small steeple on the roof where Kat's bubble popped, but it was okay, because they settled into Jesus' loving arms, and they were home.

CONCLUSION

Kat's Magic Bubble had two endings. I had to write the one that came to be.

One night the call came that the hospital had received a heart that was a match for Kat.

But unfortunately, things in life don't always turn out as planned. Despite the best efforts of a wonderful staff of doctors and nurses, and a valiant struggle on Kat's part, seven days later, we let Kat go home.

Once at each hospital we were asked if we should let her go. Until the last time, when Kat was 5 1/2 years old, we always said no, but I often wondered if we should have let her go when she was born.

But children are strong; they never give up. Kat could always see the magic on even the darkest days. Her love and courage and joyful spirit will always be with us.

AUTHOR BIO

Jeff Lower was born and raised in Moose Lake, Minnesota. At the age of ten, he began working at his family's indoor and outdoor movie theaters in Moose Lake. After graduating from high school, Jeff attended the Duluth Business School. He gained additional experience by working in St. Paul, Minnesota restaurants while attending a quantity foods school there.

A desire to combine his love of skiing and travel with work resulted in a move to Colorado where Jeff worked at a ski resort in the Rocky Mountains. Later, Jeff returned to Moose Lake, working at various local restaurants and for the city's street department.

Jeff's grandparents owned a livery stable business in Moose Lake before a fire destroyed the town in 1918. Realizing that automobiles were fast replacing the horse-and-buggy, they built the city's first theater in 1919 on the site of their livery stable. Jeff now manages the family's current theater, built in 1936.

Jeff enjoys fishing, hunting, and the outdoors with his wife and son. He's always been interested in writing, but *Kat's Magic Bubble* is his first book. Jeff feels his experience in the theater business has helped him with his writing.

ILLUSTRATOR BIO

Pegi Ballenger was born and grew up in Houston, Texas. She graduated with a Bachelor of Fine Arts degree from Newcomb College of Tulane University in New Orleans, Louisiana. After continuing her education with classes in commercial art, radio, and television, Pegi worked as a copywriter, advertising director, and continuity director for television. In addition to illustrating children's books, her paintings have shown in art galleries in Texas, Colorado, and Minnesota where she has also taught adult and children's art classes. Pegi works in a variety of media from dry pastels to computer graphics. Most of her work is representational with strong color and high contrast. Favorite subjects are people (especially children), animals, and landscapes. Pegi, her husband Ray, and a long-haired dachshund live in Woodland Park, Colorado. You can visit her website at:

http://pegiballenger.efoliomn1.com

TO ORDER ADDITIONAL COPIES OF

Kat's Magic Bubble

or other Savage Press Books

Call

1-800-732-3867

or

E-mail:

mail@savpress.com

Purchase copies online at
www.savpress.com

Visa/MC/Discover/American Express/
ECheck are accepted via PayPal.

All Savage Press books are available through all chain
and independent bookstores nationwide.
Just ask them to special order if the title is not in stock.